# CERTIFIABLE

Other books by PAMELA MORDECAI

Poetry
*Journey Poem*
*De Man: a Perfomance Poem*

Anthologies
*Jamaica Woman* (with Mervyn Morris)
*From Our Yard: Jamaican Poetry Since Independence*
*Her True-True Name* (with Betty Wilson)

Reference
*Culture and Customs of Jamaica*
(with Martin Mordecai)

# Certifiable

**PAMELA MORDECAI**

For Lynne!

Thanks so much for coming.
Here's to "unrepentant
livity"! Warm & good
wishes,

Pam

29 NOV 2001

Cover photograph: Eyewire.
Book design by Julie Scriver.
Printed in Canada by AGMV Marquis.
10  9  8  7  6  5  4  3  2  1


Canadian Cataloguing in Publication Data

Mordecai, Pamela
Certifiable

Poems.
ISBN 0-86492-295-7

I. Title.

PS8576.O6287C47  2001      C811'.54      C2001-900271-8
PR9199.3.M6358C47    2001


Published with the financial support of the Canada Council for
the Arts, the Government of Canada through the Book Publishing
Industry Development Program, and the New Brunswick Culture
and Sports Secretariat.


Goose Lane Editions
469 King Street
Fredericton, New Brunswick
CANADA E3B 1E5

*for my sisters Mary Cresser and Betty Wilson*

# Contents

**Acknowledgements**

# JUS A LIKL LOVIN

## Tell Me

So tell me what
you have to give:

I have strong limbs
to haul in castaways
stomach to swallow time
digest the days
salt skin to sail on smooth
like morning sea and tangy
lips for kissing.

I'm well fixed
for all love's traffic.

And further, I've an ear
open around the clock
you know, like those phone
numbers that you call
at any time. And such soft eyes
that smile and ferret out
the truth. Extraordinary eyes
and gentle – you can see yourself.

It's strong and warm and dark,
this womb I've got, and
fertile: you can be a child
and play in there, and if
you fall and hurt yourself
it's easy to be mended.

I know it sounds a little much
but that's the way it seems to me.

So tell me, brother,
What have you to give?

## Poems Grow

on window ledges or especial corners
of slightly dirty kitchens where rats hide

or offices where men above the street
desert their cyphers of the market place

to track the clouds for rain or ride the wind
guileless as gulls oblivious of the girl

upon the desk who proffers wilting breasts
for a fast lunch.        Ah which of us wants

anything but love? And first upon the hill-
side where bare feet in a goat's wake

avoiding small brown pebbles
know earth as it was made

and women working fields
releasing cotton from the mother tree

milking teats heavy with white
wholesomeness or riding wave

on wave of green cane till
the swell abates and the warm

winds find only calm brown surfaces
thick with the juicy flotsam of the storm

make poems

and men who speak the drum bembe
dundun conga dudups cutter

or blow the brass or play the rhumba box
or lick croix-croix marimba or tack-tack

and women who record all this
to make the tribe for start in blood

send it to school to factory to sea
to office university        to death

make poems

and we who write them down
make pictures intermittently

(sweet silhouettes fine profiles
a marked face) but the bright light

that makes these darknesses
moves always always beyond mastery

Griot older than time on Zion Hill
weaving a song into eternity.

## Shooting the Horses
*for Martin Manley*


At dawn he rose early again
and went after the horses.
He traps them manes glowing
ripe tangerine like Tintoretto
apocalypse horses-of-morning

snap-snap with his little
black box shoots the world
as it was the first day
green gold with strong legs
and a mane to be tossed
and the damp Mona plains
to be eaten like fire.

And what do you seek
my beloved, in the seed
of the day, when the tenderest
leaf of green light breaks
the earth of the dark?

What coin pulls you
wet from me, clutching
your little machine
obliging you capture
the crucified trees, their crosses
of shadows haunting
the rest of this Sabbath?

Is it wisdom or hope that you stalk?
Would you have me walk
with you?

Shall I sleep as you follow
the hooves of those shadows
the footprints of mountains
the musk of the mist
the tracks of the earliest earth?

I will leave you, my love.

It was Eve who first
murdered the morning.

## Dust

And so to bed: on this
sweet tropic evening
sky the colour of red coat plum
what's there to do
but go to bed?

In round about two minutes'
time three million sperm let loose
going do some rockers
here – no lime that brother
a dead serious search
for a black egg
to make into
another nigger.

Now them have many versions
of who be the
downpresser but just now
I will forward as
a heavyweight
contender for that title
this here nigger
that I'm under.

The sky dims into purple ripe
star-apple then bougainvillea fading
bleached into fragile pallor
by a relentless sun.

He's gone the sun the nigger
and I have yet to learn
the lessons of a decent chastity.
Like the trees I follow seasons
fruiting, fruiting with the coming
of the rain that I am parched for.

## Convent Girl

She was a convent girl, that's all.
Granted, arrayed against a wall
tummy tucked in tail under and
a saucy cigarette in hand,
the average self-respecting wand
inside the average room of men
would always stand and wave.
A minor talent, that, it gave
her little comfort once she knew

men liked her. Liked her. One or two
knew why. The common-herdy rest
made it a case of clump and curve
of winey waist and bubbly breast.

But sooth the girl had winkled out
the thing that made them tick.
She saw it wasn't any sexy trick
of lingering, no style of rock-
your-body, swing-your-tit
or heave-your-ass. What she
could screw so it would fit
a man was her mind's eye.

It was a dangerous oversight.

They said she was a boasie bitch
they said it really wasn't right
that such a slutty little tease

should soak up sun and feel cool breeze.
They catch her in the road one night
fuck out her life and fling her in a ditch.

She was a convent girl, that's all —
a little girl that five men fall
because she see over their head
beyond their footsole to their dread
of having passed and not been there.

She died for having felt their fear.

## To No Music

That is my quarrel with this country.
You hear them say: "April?
April? Spring's on its way, come April."
And, poor things, believe it too.
See them outside, toes blue
in some skemps little cotton skirt
well set on making what don't go so, go so.
And think: this big April morning
it make as if to snow.
Serious!

That is something that must
make a body consider: if you can't
trust the way the world turn –
winter, spring, summer, autumn –
what you can trust?

When it reach April
and you been bussing your shirt
for eight straight month just
to keep warm, you in no mood
to wait one dege-dege day more.
Not when you poor
and cold in the subway
cold in the street
cold where you work
where you eat
where you sleep.

But you don't get a peep
of protest from these
people. "Well, it's late
this year," they say, toes blue
peeping out the open-toe shoe,
and hug the meagre little skirt
tight round them, shivering
for all they worth.

They don't agree with the coldness
and they don't disagree;
they walk to no music
and that is misery.

## Sky Jazz

*Sky jazz*
*razz-ma-tazz*
*de furry white fellows raisin cane on brass*
*heavy set greys on dem big drums*
*fine black fingers strum-strum strumming de bass*
*some serious harmonics in the winds*
*and strings to tear you heart out.*

Is true you hear the notes first
but the crash surprise you anyhow
cymbals of light fat beads of liquid
sound and best and baddest on the flute
horns traps and congo drums to fall E.T.
Can't hear that sky music and don't recall
E.T.
      E.T.? E.T. is a long long story.

Classes Celina Crawford – is so
she name – come from
a town in de South name Jericho.
To this day nobody know
what vagaries of fate or frivolous
female fancy direct her shapely legs
down the stone steps of her cousin
Ephraim's Baptist church cross
three broad blocks – the road
to sure damnation – to her Uncle
Floyd's speakeasy, and her
destiny: E.T.

E.T. was a music man.
Don't play a damn thing but the fool
Classes Celina say between her teeth –
but no way she believe that. No
way that was true. Give that yellow
fellow one shot of white rum
and hear him sound a trumpet
like archangels drumming up
a new arrivant. Fetch him another lick
and him blow a bamboo stick
to give Pan-self red-eye.

E.T. have a talent – hear Classes
Celina again – it give the Almighty
a deep satisfaction to make.
The voice of a bard. A windpipe to wake
up a tune on the trumpet so
the cherubim dance. And the stomach
for liquor that take Bacchanal turn
into a Sunday school picnic.

When them reach to J.A. she declare:
No way drunk and disorderly
ruling my life over here. You see
U.S.A.? That's one kettle of fish.
Escoveitched in the sweat of my
very own skin. But is me was
determined. This love was my wish.
The best of a day of a week
of a year was to sit in Floyd's
fanning my foolish black face
and wait on your mouth

on your fingers to grace
his saloon with that sound.
Still ain't no one around
with a spirit relieving itself
like your own, Everald T.
Still ain't no man could blow
through a horn or a bone
and make up sky music like you —
but that don't help them two
little niggers tie up in my skirt.

Classes left E.T.

                He never got
over this woman. He drink
when he think how he miss
her. He drink when he think
of the two little boys that he leave
with dem head in her skirt.
And he musing on dem
and he playing in a dingy
rum bar in Rae Town.

*Down South in Jericho black folk say*
*the world turn slower when the angels dance.*
*A slow-down world keep back tomorrow*
*stretching out the joy. Extend the sorrow*
*too, is true, so if you glad you woo*
*them angels with a groovy tune.*

One old tuneless instrument
helping him bleat out his woe.

And the warders from prison
on Fleet Street not one so-so man
get up to go home. And the prisoners
down to the hardened house-
breakers look out from the brick
prison walls and they clap
and they bawl live eye water –
and beg Everald Townsend to play.

Then E.T. stone drunk stumble up to Top
Mountain come visit the children one day.
Classes say, Everald Townsend you crazy?
Not the slightest chance. No sir. No way.
You pay any mind to these children?
You send them a book or a shirt?
You know if them hungry or frighten?
You's them Puppa so I never say
worthless nor lazy nor drunk
about you. But I telling you sober
or drunk keep your tail out of here
till you walking with more than a tear
in your pants.

                    E.T. don't play one note
since that day. Move up here beside me
come capture a house. Fix up roof
put on door move in a old piano
a table two chair. Then he make
his arrangements regarding supply
of his water and power and phone.
So whenever time E.T. phone home
is my line that him take for him own –

same like him commandeer
my water pipe and hijack
my electric wire.

Still no day don't go by
but he making his way
up to Allman Hill School
to watch by the playfield
and grin at the two yellow
pikini romping in dirt.
And Classes get into a stew
if she reckon his shape
on the road, if she glance
him inside the bus shelter
saving his frame from the rain.

E.T. don't have a chance.
Liquor end de romance.
White rum cripple him finger.
Sky music going linger
forever inside of him throat . . .

## Caliban Calypso or Original Pan Man

*for Kamau Brathwaite*

CHORUS
*And too we come from island*
*So we know you Prospero*
*Fancy yourself as high priest*
*Sporting cape and wand and so*

*Serve up you so-so pikni*
*As a sacrifice*
*Because you want your kingdom back*
*No mind the price*

*You never give the girl a chance*
*To organize she own romance*
*You fraid Miranda get to understand*
*That the island man-of-words is Caliban.*
*You fraid Miranda get to understand*
*That the shaman man-of-words is Caliban.*


I
On high hillsides or as he floats
over the blue in small bright boats
see homo Caribbeanis grin
at how he's fecund, revelling in
how the ting-ting can spring
the fire in him wire still crackling.

"So, how much pikni you make, man?"
Him can't answer you back
but him quick to tell you
woman is a leggo-beast – "so slack!"

CHORUS


II
And Sycorax? Perhaps
each island woman
mated and devastated
by some regional ramgoat
persuaded that the family plan
is a conspiracy to kill black man?

See her in travail with her lot
She's had them out –
they're all she's got
her witchery the alchemy
to conjure food inside a pot.

CHORUS


III
Of course, till now we don't determine
who insprignant Sycorax
a matter upon which the bard
not giving any facts. Hole in
him head as far as any memory of that.

But if you check the niggergram
the chat have it to say
is backra massa rape her
put her in the family way.

CHORUS


IV
As for the creole boy child
him tongue twining with curses?
Muttering glossalalic nonsenses
him find him can decline
him pain in verses, start spirits with words,
and the birds, if him call dem, will come.

When him listen, him heart flutter
for him hear the crying stones;
the rattle of creation waking
bones reaching for bones.

The sound prickle him body,
it make him head start rise;
him bruck a stick and clean it off
and start lick galvanize.

CHORUS

V

So man when the music reach you
and the rhythm start take hold
and you feel the need to bring
the little chap in from the cold

consider meditation
and the fruits that it can bring
remember breed and grind
is two very different someting.

*And too we come from island*
*So we know you Prospero*
*Fancy yourself as high priest*
*Sporting cape and wand and so*

*Serve up you so-so pikni*
*As a hapless sacrifice*
*Is want you want your kingdom back*
*No matter what the price*

*So poor Miranda never understand . . .*
*But you better know say that we understand*
*That the island man-of-words is Caliban!*
*So we jumping when we hear him playing pan*
*For we love that man-of-words, that Caliban.*

## Will's Flowers
*for David*


I never yearned for snow
though brand new clothes from fat
Sears-Roebuck catalogues
committed to the U.S. post
by Uncle Lannie's faithful hand
in Cincinnati's never never land –
those made me glad enough.
He stayed away for years
writing Aunt V long letters
casting box after box onto
the dead slow sea-mail waters
hoarding expiring pennies
for a car a house storing
for ever after the best time
of his life. Adult and old
I never thought, "Is how
him manage foreign? Not
a wife. No family, no kin."
And so of course I follow him.

Now when spring reach T.O.
and the wild blonde from up
the street that tend to endless
cats and her small garden
with fierce care come forth
with spade in hand to set
again this year pot upon
pot of yellow daffodils

I think how we ex-slaves
enfranchised manumitted
free of snow white queens
Britannic motherland
I think we still don't
understand the bard's
peregrinations and sake
of that we dis poor Will
mightily do him wrong.

Niggers still coming North
lured by the siren song
of work and decent pay
the chance to quarry out
a little life. Meanwhile
as dog nyam dog cold
carving up your carcass
vampire cops hunt you
for your dark blood this skip
of light this skemps of flower
that God promote from grass
rooted in blackness bent
on breaching ice just
pushing pushing up to
celebrate sun summer
unrepentant livity.

To rass! What a misguided fuss.
The blasted daffodils is just like us.

**That Time of Year**
*for Chou and Mei*


It is that time of year.
I know because Mei Ling
(a refugee from the
Imperial Court fallen
on meagre times and therefore
boarded with island poor
relations) this facety dog
done left ceramic tile
long time capture my chair –
the one half-decent armchair
in the house.

I think I need to say
before the story tell:
my daughter will not take
her dog to see the canine
cosmetologist –
no mind I say I'll pay.
So sake of that the dog
perambulate and
pick up every piece of
sin and litter that come
in her way.

                    Just now I study
her repose. Generous
bangs of shih-tzu hair
above her eyes stitch seeds

of cosmos to her facial fuzz.
I see her stir make a small
growl a snarly snarl and then
subside again to jelly-
belly rise and fall of sleep.
I kiss my teeth. Another deep
stuck-up inscrutable Chiney
for us brown mongrelkind
to tolerate. Just make
her wait. Year after next
is a entire new age.

To tell God's truth though
I get a buzz considering
that in this age's final century's
anno penultimo
some part of next spring's
fancy breeds in a dog's
visage slinks in her paws
winds into skimpy strands
of rasta locks upon her front.

And now she bounds to ground
and stalks in germinating
beauty towards the stairs.
As she ascends the cosmos seed-
lets fall – a fount of yellow
pink and purple tears.

**Lottery**
*for Kim, Jeremy and Daniel, born 27 August 1974*


An old lady lighting her way
with lotteries: Six Forty-nine
Wednesday and Saturday and
Super Seven ("Is a better deal")
each Friday night.

                    "You really
tink you going to win dat ting?"
Miss Ida quarrels amiably
down from the sagging balcony
above her own. She smiles immersed
in memories:
                    . . . a jam jar full
of grains of rice small seeds spilled out
on a huge tray counted and then
refilled and then counted again
for one whole day Papa
and Uncle Lan consumed
with counting up and setting down
and averaging a dozen counts
to find the number of rice grains
inside the jar . . .

And guess what? Is no win them win!
A bonafide washing machine
Pa's salary for one whole month
decked with a bow red white and blue
arrive imperial at our gate.

"There's method to this winning thing."
Raising her voice for benefit
of Ida's ears, she waves a hand
that hardly rises more than so.

She knows but Ida doesn't know
how many years she's lived-and-bought,
times weeks, times three. She also knows
the odds (Kevin her youngest gran
found them somewhere he calls
the world wide web). He says
each week she pares them down.

She's used to wearing things away
and since hugging her skinny knees
she heard her first Anansi tale
swaddled in starlight and cool breeze
and saw that crafty spider spin frail
deadly traps, she's known the world's a web.
(Seeing as he's young it's news to Kev.)

And on the day Kev's dad was born
three women carrying on their road
(a short street with ten yards or so)
put down their babies like one load.

And so it is. You never know
how the threads twine how the world go.
You try your hand you take your chance.
When Massa God play music
you make sure you rise to dance.

## Deadly Beauties

Hear Dot's voice on the phone
doing its best not to bray:
What you say? A X-ray?
And you need it *today*?
*And* a mammo as well?
Don't take serious thing make play.
You well know when tings tough,
is all four month delay!

Oh, all right. Since is you
I'll see what I can do.
Maybe you can get through
on the last of the month.
Try your luck. No break-
fast, you hear. And you better
prepare to spend the whole day.
Take good note of the date.
Do you best to reach early –
it can shrivel the wait.

By the way, is five thousand
dollar – don't holler. You
hearing me right. And no
cheques, please. Raw cash in your
hand. Doctor Freddie, he
says I must not trust a
soul. Too much handwritten
money is funny these days.

Well, it's nice that my doc
has his procedures straight.

I don't drink. I don't joke
around drugs. I don't smoke
no strange weed, don't let no
foreign buddy poke into my body.
But this virtue hard won
is rectitude moot
cause the big C is blind.
It don't care if you shoot
or you sniff or imbibe –
it's a catholic plague.

And thank God until now
I still get the best news:
Radiologist Fred
says he don't see a thing
in the shots mesmerizing
me on the small screen.
Still his love note will say
as it does every time:
Girl, you must test your breasts.
Search their thick ropy nests
for the tiniest lump.
If you don't hunt that bump
don't blame me if that baby
pop up on this screen as a teen
or a growth that can vote.

There is times I could wring
that fat man's flabby throat.

So it's me here alone
with these bumper crop tits.
I still don't shove and push them.
I'm the most patient sinner.
When the verdict arrives canker
worm's made them dinner
I will hear it one minute
one day in due course.

Till that time and that season
can't see one rhyme or reason
to torture us three every day.
Enough once a year fear
should have its free rein.

So I say, Thanks a lot,
Dot. See you Friday, D.V.

And we hang up and sigh –
Deadly beauties and me.

## Jus a Likl Lovin

All up and down this
plain of Liguanea
the Mona moon heaving
up from the sea
it have some village
ram some likl girls
that not long leave behind
them hot-comb curls . . .
The big man village
ram-them making press
don't give the likl
gyal-pikni no rest.

The girls don't know father
nor grandpapa. Most times
them not much younger
than them ma – fifteen
is not much time. Love is
a dance hall song loud
on the radio a sharp
clap cross the jaw
if they're lucky
and stern instruction:
"Go and learn your book.
You want to look like me
before you turn twenty?"
The clap burning them skin
them hold them jaw and cry.
All dem looking

is jus a likl lovin.

Now if nuns raise you
never and forever are
familiar texts. At seven
you can appoint
occasions of sin, by ten
you recognize them as men.
By twelve you have rehearsed
taxonomies of mis-
demeanour tactics
strategies man-
oeuvres terms of truce.

Still often in the end
not much of this is any use.
If man press you is either yes
you telling him, or no.
Say yes, likl from now
them say you easy.
Say no them say
that you cock-teasy.
No way to win. And
talk the truth all
a gyal-pikni want

is jus a likl lovin.

So don't she have
to give in?

Her belly getting big.
At school them all
talking behind them hand.
"Is fool she fool to 'low
any old man to fall
her so. Nobody tell her
rubber sell at shop?"

Never mind them.
The bupsy drop
her in him car collect
her when bell ring.
She know is not a thing
but envy why them chat
her and she know
not one of them have
any place to go
but up this street. Is only
time before them meet
them daddy with him sweet
mouth and him sin
against the sixth.

Sister okay. Betwixt her two
fat thighs there's nothing
but a sluice for making pee.
That's how church
has defined her sanctity.
That's how them preach
it out to all like me.

Or maybe she was
just a lucky chick
and found some loony
guy who gave her free
without her giving in

jus a likl lovin.

# MY SISTER MUSE

## Elizabeth

And as for you
Elizabeth
so wise
of the
slow eyelids
slower eyes
even now
secrets
grow mouldy
in your
store:
your small
foot
not quite
ready
gait
travels
with more
than I
can gather
yet we two
waxed
parallel
one heart
one head
fighting
about the
line drawn
down

the middle
of the
bed.

## My sister muse

My sister makes strange jewelled things
pieces exquisite of night and the first
light of morning selects a shoe-
black for good medicine and the heart
blood red of it chooses
small stones for the world
is made of them raids the grass
for dew with her proboscis
sucks indigo blue from the trench
of a sinkhole in Troy
on a throne of white coral nearby
a boy peels bananas
she stitches him in.
She loops round the curve of the harbour
today it is grey ah this
is the weather for fish! Bright corpses
king parrot blue chub and pink salmon
alarum the bay they are dynamite
dead.
         Astride an iguana
her hands on its fine spiny comb
she brings home their bodies
they will rest in the weave
in the sleeves of her bodice
the folds of her skirts.
My sister goes twice round the earth
she brings monsoons tornadoes
and three hurricanes the barometer
drops she hoots through the tops

of the trees she howls
in the hollows of hands
in the caves the graves
keep their dead sleep.

She weeps for the sadness of parting.

She is starting to spin.

## My sister takes over

For the first born rites
for the next born rigmarole

In the cellar under our house
our first house the house I
first remember even
nannys would hurry from
their delicate ditches
of fine dust the fattest
nannys hurling themselves
at her, "Come take me take
me beg you control me
I Nanny the Elusive
welcome captivity
if is you a take me."

The rest of us collect
ants carefully expertly
crush them roll just one
down into a nanny hole
eyes glued to the depression
like is relief supplies
or enemy attack
we waiting for watching
to see a little spurt
of dirt then Bam! we slam
the empty condensed can
cage of captivity
into the hole scoop up

the bottom –
                    always a
little fine dust with luck
a nice fat nanny.

Till this day she a capture
the choicest loot the fattest
plunder all God she take
wind round her likl finger
no bother waste no bet
no bother fret anything
my sister ask for she get.

Who come first come first
who come next do your best
or do your worst just don't
come first.

And my soul and your soul
and the whole blessed
world of shapes and savours
delicate weather fine
feathered or furry things

discriminately carved
intricate patternings
all earth all heaven soured
sickened putrified
by a mere place inside
the scheme of things.

For the first born rites
for the next born rigmarole.

## My sister gets married

It is dark

At five she is stirring
catarrh'd in wet coughs
of old whiskered wives
assembled for rites black
bumps draped in blankets
astride sturdy boxes
knees knitted together
heel out and toe in
securing the bride for
them brazen can't finish
these days . . .

My sister gets up and
she walks to the window
in an ocean of sky
sees the crazy old crabs

She opens the window
and smiles clouds feel bad
embarrassed like how them
dress drab and bedraggled

Crabs curl into their backs
wrap shawls gainst cool breeze
gainst the pride of the morning
pat safe in them bosom
nuff thread bag containing

queen gold and king silver
for blood is the sign them can
leave go dead quiet

Beyond in the yard is
the one she will mate with
she measures his limbs feels
the stems of his arms as
they wrap her slight body
his trunk as it tumbles
cut down by her eyes

My sister is wise
she will give herself
to him little by little
he'll pole up the stream
of her hauling so patient
work his craft to the head
spring exploring the way
then reckless on rapids
romp with the river

Crabs bless the new blood
leave the money for wares
bedsheet with embroidery
new ewer and basin
big enamel chimmey
coal pot some flat iron
a plaque for declaring
the Lord is the head of
this house breaking bread
with the household

eavesdropper divine
every God time
you open your mouth . . .

My sister looks down
at her small sturdy body:
sees herself long years later
black bump of a crab
reposed on a box
with a threadbag of silver
and rheum in her eyes.

## My sister cries the sea

My sister is crying and crying
her tears grow to salt stormy showers
to rain and to rapids and rivers
they run to the sea to the sea.

My sister sobs softly she knows
she listens at shells and the shoals
she hears from fish sleeping at nightfall
she gathers from mushrooms and moulds.

Hears walking fish clear at Mayaro
black eyes popping out of their heads:
"The wind it gone out of the water
the sea things is tarred to their beds."

Hears lichen and moss at Newcastle
as tree things brown up and go dry:
"The poisons them capture the air waves!
The land and the sea going to die."

My sister is crying and crying.
Her tears have joined up with the tide.
The shells and the shallows have vanished.
The earth and the heavens divide.

## My sister Gloria
*for M*

i
So tell me girl who going to bring
you praise going raise up
any allelu for you?


ii
Just like the Magic Man
whose fancy handwork
almost drowned your first

big birthday-party day:
you in pink organdy
a crown of coralita

in your hair stretching from
Mama's lap Mama furloughed
from mania by powders

for this amber afternoon
to steady you as you manoeuvre
Grandpère's ritual translation:

a fête to get the family
(for that read all of Harbour View)
acquainted with his latest gran.

I see you stretching out
for gold: a coin plucked from
this Mandrake's ear offered

between pursed thumb and index
finger then – poof, wave of wand –
obliterated. Gone. Not there.


iii
Chile how I live to wish
them wands stashed firmly into
underpants! Please God the tears

you shed that time stood in
for those you should have bawled
this year your fortieth to heaven

when man home family
the whole catastrophe
collapse just so. Not you

though. That is just not you.
Instead, your eyeball dry
as January dust. No powder

helping you you answer
musts of where to go who
to entrust with deadly

secrets ghosts of which one
did which deed to who
so long ago . . .


iv
So, who going praise?

Me girl. I raise the toast.
I say you hail. I bow
to mischief moulting
in your eye to punning
purple in your mouth
to steering wheels spun
with panache to fuck-
yous flung at motor hogs
and pedals floored
under your feet.

To getting on
with getting on.

More time for you, say I,
more time and thanks
and tears
and toasts and
tintinabulations.

For every bit of praise
is meet.

## My two sisters take a bath

1 Verna

*Oh is grass today*
*oh is grass today*
*but it not going stay*
*so the Bible say.*
*Oh, is trash tomorrow*
*Oh, is trash tomorrow*
*so me looking for the*
*nother nother day.*

That is Verna the one crazy
lady in Almond Tree Grove
singing as she untie
the bundle of dry
banana leaves she use
to wrap her small things in.

She wash in the still pool
by Moses Rock each morning
at nine for the last seven
years so now is a rite
for all the little
elementary school
boy pikni to stand up
(dangerous) behind a
dread line of dildo
and gaze on Verna in her
splendid nothingness:

                      her head

a crown of kinky grey
carefully combed each day
with her fine fingers her rage
resplendent only here
not a sign of age anywhere
on the rest of her body.

So generations of small men
stare in perpetual wonder
as she disappear right down
the water covering her hair
the ripples dimpling out-
ward till the pool resume
its even countenance
still as death. As one they
hold their breath          as one
they sigh when Verna's fore-
head break the mirror pool
and sky cloud trees
and granite Moses Rock
shatter and multiply
about neck shoulder hip
breast belly thigh.

*Oh is grass today*
*oh is grass today*
*but it not going stay*
*so the Bible say.*
*Oh, is trash tomorrow*
*Oh, is trash tomorrow*
*so me looking for the*
*nother nother day.*

Bell ring. A line of little
wiser men spill from the cacti
bleeding red fruit flowers
dodge cow pats climb
two by two the concrete stairs
and sit to drill their tables
seven times seven.
                    "Whoever
hear a River Mumma sing
follow her to the heaven
kingdom of the sea."




2 Patsy


*Riddle me this, riddle*
*me that. Guess me this riddle —*
*and perhaps not. Now man,*
*man always following*
*this thing around. Sometime*
*it stand up and sometime*
*it sit down but no matter*
*day or night him always*
*following it around.*

Patsy is a town gyal.
She bathe under a pipe
in the yard of the convent
on Delacree Road every day,
surrender every stitch

62

upon her back to wash
(always the decent woman)
her body and her clothes.

Nobody know how
Patsy come by it (bar
Almighty providing)
but she always have soap.
So flagging the barbed-
wire fence to one side
of the convent, behold:
three panty two brassiere
two slip (narrow) two (wide)
and the three skirt and four
blouse she wear at one time.

Patsy herself screaming
clean is sitting naked
in the sun on the steps
of the little convent chapel
say she drying out.

*Riddle mé this, riddle
me that. Guess me this riddle —
and perhaps not. Now man,
man always following
this thing around. Sometime
it stand up and sometime
it sit down but no matter
day or night him always
following it around.*

No girl at the high school
can resist Patsy's lore
is more education
than they ever hoped for.
She speaks upon the finer
points of mathematics
economics, zoo and botany.
Upon these subjects she
is more clear than any prof
in any university.

She pop a bit of Spanish
too with style and French
of the expletive kind. No
niñas here can fathom how
they say she's lost her mind.
In fact they find her mind
clearly abounds. Not one
soul up and down these holy
grounds is half as plain
or to their thinking
half as sane.

On men and madness
though Patsy is best.

*Riddle me this, riddle*
*me that. Guess me this riddle —*
*and perhaps not.*

## My sister red

My sister's supporting
the wall of the Jewish
Community Centre
on the south side of Bloor
at Spadina. She watches
the man cross the road
with a face like old snow.
He stares back like he's viewing
the Devil's own sibling.
She observes him disposing
of *Outreach* a poor people's
paper that retails for a dollar.
She sees he is selling
to one somebody maybe
in maybe a hundred that
passing him by. She smile
a small smile and she sigh a
a small sigh, and she sips.
It is balm to her lips.

My sister is higher
than jets kites and eagles
these hell-blazing days.
Gloss that all of the ways:
unfolded she stands
above six feet tall
the length of her body
a tortured intestine
an organ that guzzles

her life an intricate
folding unfoldable fife
whimpers in trembles out
like shame-lady bush if
you take your foot touch it.
That sweet locomotion
mount a horse mount a man
bearing down for a child.

Too, my sister is wild
lit up bright with Labatt's
Red Stripe Red Deer Red Dog
any-old-craven canine
with scour-belly moonshine
for sale. Regard her outside?
Not a sign that the rot's
got her brain. She's a woman
aglow with a rain
of black hair that just
stirs in the burp of
the subway's hot air
as it spurts from a grate.
Not a wrinkle has scratched
at her cheek or her brow
not a tremor has snatched
at her hands: they grip like
crab louse.

Uplifted, she is.
Yea, the last of her house
she is hearing the winds
swish-swish cross the plains

hundreds of acres of years.
She is seeing the mammoths
the mastodons die. She is
watching the lie of the land
as it shifts the drifts
of the dunes. Her body
a tepee the infant
asleep many moons.

Now many folk agree
is sake of types like she
and types like me hijacking
the provincial treasury –
is we make the budget
can't balance. In more
common parlance
minorities screw up
the numbers. Which is
true. The average
migrant family does be
more than two point three.
But you see the red girl? She
don't come from nowhere.
She always was here.

Still mountain still water
still spirit run deep.

The man sells an *Outreach*.
A snort says my sister's asleep.

## My sister goes off

*On a hillside not far away*
*dawns the everlasting day.*
*Brothers, sisters, gather round,*
*Who was lost has now been found.*


i
It did not matter that
my sister Marie was a
child of the bourgeoisie,
when she went

                                             off

she boiled things down
to the least, but

                      "No not common
                      by no means common . . ."

denominator.

When God give singing out
Marie don't get, but she
don't let that fret her.
She singing all the time –
the same one song. Till Mama,
patience very self, beg
her, "Lord sake, child –
give the tune a break."

ii
When Marie ask for her damask,
we know that trouble set:

> "Somebody, run quick, na
> and get Miss Marie damask?"

That is another sign:
she talking 'bout herself like
she is some foreign body.

When the cloth come, she
smooth it flat, then point.

> "Look. See? Some little
> marks. Some idiot gold . . ."

> "Them can't come out, ma'am.
> Iron mould — to mark the
> years, tea parties, tears . . ."

> "You try
> some lime?"

> "Plenty time, ma'am.
> Them marks there will not budge."


iii
Dissatisfied, she turn
again to the napkin,
insert one panty, one

brassiere, one T-shirt
and the same one skirt.
Then fold the corners tie
a knot secure the bundle
on a stick she break from
off the lignum vitae tree.

Nobody want to take
the news to Ma:

> "Come quick, ma'am. See
> Miss Marie she . . .
>
> > gone off again!"

iv
Every time they sent me
to follow her — never the boys.

> "She is your sister, dear.
> The boys cannot appreciate
> Maria's eccentricities."

The niggergram was left
to own that verily

> "The girl child mad, just plain
> crazy. So them stay — one crack
> fambily. Suppose you meet
> her mother? Much less her
> granny — up to her great-gran!

Is so them coolie hair hang straight,
is so them brain-part obscurate."


v

Walking a ways behind
my manic sis her back-
sides counting each bump in
its turn, I mounting
supplications.

> "God, please. Don't make her do
> no foolishness. Three rosaries
> I promising, if she don't jump
> in front no bus, don't tumble
> from no bridge."


vi

Then one red afternoon
Marie take off for true.
Into a taxi. No, not
for a ride. Walk straight
in front the car. It make
she fly way up the sky,
turn pupalick. Time the man
stop the cab, come out to see
what madness make she
step before she look, Marie

done gone.

"Marie Lattibeaudaire,
second child of Charles and Claire,
died tragically yesterday,"
the *Gleaner* said. "An accidental
death, caused by a fatal blow
resulting from a chance
encounter with a hand-
some (yes, so it say, a handsome) cab."


vii
Twenty! The girl was plenty young.
Now nough time when I working late
night squeaking with coquis
I swear I hear the porch
complaining for her weight,
and then, clear-clear, I hear her song.

*On a hillside not far away*
*dawns the everlasting day.*
*Brothers, sisters, gather round,*
*Who was lost has now been found.*

# CERTIFIABLE

## Walker

My mother
was a walker
clothes in a brown
paper bag headed ·
for where under
some car some
bus some
precipice
her whimsy
claimed
a place.

It ran
in the family:
her father
walked one morning –
just so – down
into the sea
left Grandma
with eleven crosses.
Small wonder
(my man says)
he did it.
Poor Grandpa
cut his losses.

## No Breaks

No breaks in you not even cracks
no fragmentations pasted-backs
no little nicks no fleshy sags
no dark eyes sporting puffy bags.

Some tiny flaw would cheer me so.
It's such a ragged way I go
it's such a ragged way I've been
who'd think that you and I were kin?

I've railed I've prayed I've took to bed
I've swallowed pills and smeared my head
with VapoRub and Tiger Balm –
and still I hound capricious calm.

No breaks in you no signs of wear
no worry marks for us to share.
I'll trudge this way alone I guess
praying for you each day, Oh bless
her with a little mess,
Oh Lord, a little mess . . .

## The Angel in the House

First January find me here
considering this writer
who glad that she inherit
five hundred pound a year
so she could choke a Angel
in her House. No sooner than
the Spirit dead, she feel
she can inscribe exactly
what she please at any time
she please, being as how
she now decide she safe
inside this room for just
she-one.

      Well, to start with,
I feel this sister mean.
Whole world of somebody
pile up on top them one
another and she out
looking wider berth for
she alone? Nobody
tell her all o' we cramp
up out here struggling for
abbreviated air?

You say she mad? You say
is mad she say *she* mad?
So tell me where to find
any sane body these

dread days when every soul
outside them skull walking
and talking to themself
a raving recitation.

As for the Cherub
I feel it for this Spirit who
ten chance to one just
never had no choice
but had to put sheself
into a house accept
the job to jook and cook
to clean and care for man
and pikni pot and pan.

This Miss Woolf take a simple
view of pum-pum politics,
she make a crass construction
of the sweet domestic life.
She don't know Wife is just
another way to make it
through?

        I feel this getty-getty
attitude passing obscene.
I feel this own-room business
smack of Mistress Queen.
I feel this graceful space
for croquet and the season's
change wide hats and flailing
arms and cool white beauty
and Leonard let's arrange

for Vita to be here
till spring hijack disgrace
and take it pretty far.

And say for argument
she feel that she must go
another way, she have no
cause to wring the Spirit neck!
Don't that must summon serried
ranks of the angelic hosts?
Set them upon the path
to war? Don't that must be
a clarion call to all the ghosts
of women wearied into
time by tendering?

Is who she think she be?

Gloom get her in the end.
At home we'd say selfish —
so Angel Duppy come
claim she.

        I say House Angel
make her play — baking
babies and fine embroidery.
She plant her one small
talent and it bear.
Miss Woolf she make a
follow-fashion move behind
a bird manoeuvring
in circles never noticing

the circles narrowing
with each fly past.

The end, old people say,
of such a route is
penetration of your
own lugubrious ass.

## Blessed Assurance

*for Louise Bennett*

Every day I take my time
to reach to this subway
and moved by the Spirit
seek some little space
corner or elevation
from which I send up
the day's offering.

Trust I trust the Lord
to lay a precious word upon
my lips and praise His Holy
Name I glad to relate to date
He do not fail me. Alleluia.
Hail the Soon-Coming King.
Amen.

Not a morsel of food
pass my lips since I wake
but man liveth not
from bread alone but by each
word that break anointed
from God mouth.

Black people not easy though —
that is God truth as well!
You would think from how white
people sauce us since we walk off
those ship we would know is

hand holding hand that see we
survive these many historical years.

I don't come here dirty nor stink.
True, I not young no more
and can tell you for sure
things is hard for old people
these days. But my mother
God bless her tell we from
we small:

"Two thing I could promise
you lot: tomorrow
and the day after. Make sure
you keep breathin' – pull in
and blow out – and the prize
you go win is old age.
Is reward more than wealth
but make no mistake
is a terrible stage in your life."

"When you open you mout
you find spit shower out
'stead of word, you can't hold
your pee when you sneeze,
and your knees giving out
when you climb up two stair.
Your nose don't work well
so every God-thing fair
or foul it smell the same way."
So she train we from then.

"Young is easy," she say,
"the wages of sin is old age."

So I following Ma and I
coming here clean corpse
and clothes. What I wear true
is old but it clean and it suiting
the weather. And I carry myself
as my mother prescribe from
them days, with appropriate pride.

So who you would think
cut the wickedest eye
when them passing me by?
Don't you know is my people –
my long-chupsing bounce-batty people!
Dressed for sin and destruction
devoid of instruction
hell bent on the Devil own path!

Still I stay for as long as man
woman or chile coolie chiney
black white I don't care
will linger to hear me.
If the Lord Jesus come before
I am called this is where
he sure going to find me.
I speak in the hope that even
one passing body have a mind
to consider the call to repentance
in these latter days. That even
one so-so backslider

will change him bad ways
relinquishing all deadly sin.
That one prodigal find
him way back to him Pa
who longing to let us all in.

Is the last train so I going home
ever speaking my word as I go:
"Roam ye not in unrighteousness
for the yoke is easy and
the burden light and the time
for conversion is now while
you might while the bright
of the Lord is upon us,
before the last darkening days.
Repentance, my brothers and sisters!
Repentance and prayers and praise."

## Serafina

October nineteen ninety-three
when God tell Serafina that
the world going end soon-soon, poor
woman frighten little most she pee
her drawers. Fina (for everybody
call her so) Fina and Eurith
walking by the hospital on
Schuter Street when Fina halt
spectacles hypnotised
by two small of-no-colour eyes
inside a ratty pointed squirrel
head. Talk truth squirrel look less
alive than dead his moulting
fur baring blots of pink skin
sparse wilting tail and slowly
mumbling mouth. "The thing,"
Fina declare, her finger trembling
as she point, "The thing," she say again,
less faltering, "is talking clear
as day, talking  to me!"

So Fina heard God's voice from out
the mouth of a small beast.

She share with Eurith first:
"Eurith, you's close to me
like family," she say, "and so
I feel I could explain to you.
You see day before yesterday

when I tell you the little
mangy squirrel talk to me?"
Eurith nod yes. "I going to tell
you what him say" – she look at Eurith
threatening and supplicatory
and then she let it out: "Squirrel
tell me that God Almighty
say is not long now until
Him Son come back to claim
Him world." Eurith stop braps,
grab Fina by her two shoulder:
"Listen, Fina. I not doubting
you hear from God. Don't even
doubt that squirrel talk for Him
for His ways are mysterious
and I well know is not for us
to study Him. But Fina you
must not tell nobody that
squirrel bring God message come.
Mark my word, if you talk your mind
them going to send the fellows in
white coat to lock you up."

It never stop Fina. She do
exactly as squirrel instruct,
for she and he consulting now
consistently. She hand out
tract. She pray whole day.
She preach at church, at supermarket,
on subway and the bus. She preach
to all the patients that she tend.

She tell about the squirrel too —
prophetic beast the one who bring
her the Divine advice. Till one
day a sour little man that fuss
and quarrel constantly inquire:
"Is it that all black folks are dumb
believers in this silly stuff
or is it just your one ill-bred
and poorly cultivated mind?"

Poor Fina raving she so vex:
"Corinthians one, first chapter," she
pronounce, "it dealeth with the likes
of you. The Lord shall bring to nought
the wisdom of the ones who think
them wise. And all those that bedridden
and cannot control nor piss nor poo
them bold to bring contention to all who
is vertical and continent."

Them send her home next day. Like spite
no mind she look, squirrel cannot
be found. It don't seem right
that she should lose her livelihood
for trying to carry out God's plan.
Eurith exhort her: "Good Book speak
of being wise like snake. You take
the Lord instruction and you also
take a little earthly common sense.
You really think that hardened
sinners going to understand

that God would ask a rodent with
a bushy tail to talk for him?
Only a saint would credit that."

Eurith take Serafina hat
and put it on her head. "Come chile,"
she say, "life dread I know but while
we drawing breath we doing well.
We going to look a squirrel now
a nice fat one that we can cook
or one to tell we where to look
to find a job for you."
                              The two
old friends step out into the street —
and who come prancing up to meet
them but squirrel with him half
and half top coat! Is true the bush
behind him looking thicker and
the eyes are onyx points of sense
astride his head. Fina assess
him with her gaze: "So little brute,"
she ask him, "Just exactly
what you coming now to say?"
Him take time look pon her
turning him head one side
like him well satisfy with what
him do. Then in two-twos
him flash him tail and vanish
like good news.

## Certifiable

"Grandma was certifiable,"
the infant said. "No way,"
said Grandpapa who dressed
the slice she made into
her breast two inches long
whose forehead bore a savage
bruise she dealt him with
a lignum vitae tray

"No way. She had a couple
(three or four) shall we say
breakdowns of her nerves."

"How can you tell, Grandpa,"
he asked, "when your nerves break?"
"It's when your mother cries,"
I say, "and cries and cries.
You know the times?" "And
when you smash things on
the wall?" "That's when," I say,
"that's one stretched time."

Across the houses of my mind
doors, windows bang. Something
is hatching eggs inside
my ear. It has a point
and drills (I feel it)
on the drum. No, this
is not some mania.

These are the facts. You
won't believe that things
are eating at my nose
and at my throat as well.

I loved a man of forty-two
I wished my nipple
in his mouth, his body
hard in my soft womb
my breath hot on his face.
He had a wife. My church
said No. I let him go.

I loved a man of fifty-two.
I dreamt he bore me
in his arms under a poui
pink with blooms
against a pale mauve sky.
He had a wife, he had
a son, and I am good,
so he is gone. I loved
a child of twenty-two.
He never grew.

The loves are dead.
Of no account. They stand
for all the things I want.
I want to dance. I
want to fly. To follow
rivers. Never die. I want to sing
the highest note so dogs
can hear. To stroke

the long length of the throat
of a giraffe. To laugh
till tears wash out
the pain. And laugh again.
To care for things, to make
them grow, to stay
awake until the glow
of morning covers everything.

Flies follow filth, repose
on rot. What is here
tucked between my ears
between my neck
and thighs, the flies
would celebrate.
I hate it, hate
its hot red monthly tears,
hate its puff-puff, its every-
second-breathing seething
so-insistent life. I know
like Grandmama the virtues
of a long stout knife.
And I am loose, uncertified.

## The House of Cards

i
What are you doing? Nothing.
Saving myself from madness.
It stalks me ancient legacy
queer twisted chromosome
contorted in the rainbow
of my genes. Dealing
cards reading tarots
puffing their bright dreams
my ancestors could not know
what they do. Now I sleep
sleep do nothing hide
hide from my children's friends.
Worry worry the bath
rooms are not clean.


ii
In the morning I sweep
dust build a house
of cards carefully
deck on deck at three
the children will come
brightly through the door
and blow it down
behind their father
careful chauffeur polished
shiner of their dreams
would not have noticed.

I will collect the cards
count carefully – each
pack makes fifty-three –
and put them in their box.
(I count the joker in.)
It is a curse it is a curse
but I swear it will not catch me.


iii
See her there the crazy lady
bright red striding
up the path wanting
cash for cigarettes
a cup of tea mad but
still she court the mirror
pat her head and want
hairdresser – Man I need
my hair to do and nails to paint –
I set the cards down find
ten dollars send her on her way.


iv
I go to work my eight
by eight my desk my chair
here at least no horrors fester
here at least no zombies lurk
I proofread; grave processions
black on white careful orders
of squat words.
                    Shuffling

in the corridor barest
movement on the door nothing
folded at its foot a brief missive,
"Backra lady we going put
yer bright yalla in its place."
See it stalk me backra lady
bright as Mittelholzer's music
we will burn you
we will kill you
we will will you
into dying
on the page the words
are jumbled on my head
the demon sits he is smoking
joking provoking me with pictures
of a small white space.


v
Just hold me Father
as I cook sew build
this house of cards
play hide and seek
with that twist chromosome
this is not home this place
where duppy breed
and dead provoke you
demon wink at you and poke you
dread descend and leave you cold.

vi
Is just as well I learned
this thing so long ago
what bothers me is how it grew
and bloomed and fruited
of its own volition
for that is true is absolutely true.


vii
What am I doing? Nothing.
Saving myself from madness.

## License

Papa is holding forth
to Lillibet concerning
license. On the back seat
(it's a new Hillman Minx,
colonial civil servant car
khaki below and white above)
I bounce beside myself
with olefactory transports
of brand new upholstery.

I'm listening though
for License is my love
a place of Sunday
disportation a grassy
slope for head to head and
Lillibet and me hold
hands and roll together
down the prickly hill
halting by Catholic
force of will – before hard
stone halt we. The slope
end in a concrete wall
then yards of leaking sand
teased by sometimish sea.
And bliss for me is any
day abandoned to
this License wild of salt
and rock and sand, this
drunkenness of sun and sea.

Now Papa's text concerns
adhering to the right
side of the road: "Is true
if you possess a license
(I well acquainted with
that kind: Pa's had a photo
so so old his hair was
black, a longish curl
prancing over one eye)
which means that you are free
to drive (well even I know that)
but it don't mean you drive
on any side at any speed
and stop and start reverse
and turn just as you wish!
You free to drive only
if you abide by the road code."
He look sternly at Lillibet
sidelong past her at me.
"You follow me?"

Lillibet nod. "Life is
like that," Papa resume,
"only like spite, the word
the sorry language choose
to use when man behave
as if him somehow not
obliged to heed the
regulations of the road is . . ."
Hear me shout out: "License!"

And Papa head spin round
to see what fount of force-ripe
bigger-than-her-britches
curiosity could
prompt a pikni six year
old not just to fast in older
people talk but worse
to cipher out what he
construe as elevated reasoning.

He thin his lips and make
it pass. "License is one thing
you must not confuse with liberty."

Time I was ten them figure
out, "Her head too long.
Girl children not to be
so stubborn and own-way.
She going to give her father
bellyache. You mark my word:
a thing gone bad at morning time
cannot turn good when evening
come." The consequence
of this sound apprehension
was of course that I grew
stormy as that License slope
strung out serrated shore
and here-now there-now sea.

Papa is faithful.
Drive his Caddy come
to see me every Sunday

in this place. He take time
never race to get his
visit done. Lillibet
long since gone away
to culinary school.
"She doing very well.
The lawyer say the judge
will rule about her papers
in another month or two.
God willing, she can get
to stay and make her way
in Canada."

I think of snow.
I think I couldn't go
to no cold place. I feel
sure is the sun and hill
sea spray and blue blue sky
that keep the blood racing
up to my head that keep
my two eye keen sustain
the sharpness of my ear
so I can hear better than any dog.

He smile stand kiss me
say, "I going Claire Marie.
See you next week same time
if God spare life." I watch
him go. I know I make him
grieve. Cause him new wife
and him to disagree.
But that is me. I say

I never plan to bad-drive
life. I tell him, "As I
love God, Pops, is really
life that bad-drive me."
Pops don't agree but him and
me know reasoning won't solve
this case. He got a daughter
and a fat disgrace: License
and Liberty.
                    I watch
him sink into the Cadillac
brow lowered gainst the sun.
I'm rocking gently back
and forth and back. A slab
of deal board floating out to sea.

## Acknowledgements

My work on *Certifiable* was supported by grants from the Toronto Arts Council and the Canada Council for the Arts, for which I am grateful. I would also like to thank Eddie Baugh, Jacki Brice-Finch, Kwame Dawes, Celia Ferrier, Nalo Hopkinson, Mervyn Morris, Tim Reiss, Elaine Savory, Olive Senior, Janet Sommerville, Jennifer Walcott, and Betty Wilson for encouragement and for comments on early drafts. Olive Senior made a crucial suggestion at the start of the project, D.M. Thomas nurtured its growing, and Kamau Brathwaite intervened in timely fashion at the end. I am in their debt. I am also indebted to Laurel Boone of Goose Lane Editions for her many insights and valuable suggestions. As ever, for their continued indulgence, to Martin, David, Rachel and Daniel, one love.

Many of these poems have previously appeared, some in slightly different form, in journals including *Callaloo*, *The Caribbean Writer*, *The Cincinnati Poetry Review*, *Descant*, *Graham House Review*, *Jamaica Journal*, *Kyk-over-al*, *The Literary Review*, *Matatu*, *Macomère*, *Nimrod*, *Obsidian III*, and *Savacou*, and in anthologies including *Daughters of Africa*, *Jamaica Woman*, *Eyeing the North Star: Directions in African-Canadian Literature*, *From Our Yard: Jamaican Poetry Since Independence*, *The Penguin Book of Caribbean Verse*, and *For the Geography of a Soul: Emerging Perspectives on Kamau Brathwaite*. The poems "Elizabeth" and "Walker" and a somewhat different version of "Tell Me" originally appeared in *Journey Poem* (1989).